The
Starry
Sky

Copyright © Aladdin Books Limited 1994
Designed and produced by
Aladdin Books Limited
28 Percy Street
London W1P 0LD

First published in 1995 in the United States by
Copper Beech Books,
an imprint of The Millbrook Press
2 Old New Milford Road
Brookfield, Connecticut 06804

**This edition published in 1999 by
Copper Beech Books**

Design: David West Children's Book Design
Editor: Liz White

Illustrations by Paul Doherty
Additional illustrations by Mike Lacey, Ian Thompson, Stuart Lees,
and Ross Watton - SGA
Photocredits: Pages 16 and 72: Science Photo Library; page 28: Melies (Courtesy
Kobal Collection); pages 36 and 37: Roger Vlitos; pages 8 and 55 Frank Spooner
Pictures; pages 13, 33, 41, 46 and 47 both NASA.

First published in the United Kingdom in 1994 by
Riverswift, Random House, 20 Vauxhall Bridge Road, London SW1V 2SA

Copyright in the text © Patrick Moore 1994
Dr. Patrick Moore has asserted his right under the Copyright, Designs and Patents Act,
1988, to be identified as the author of this work.

Library of Congress Cataloging-in-Publication Data
Moore, Patrick.
The starry sky / by Patrick Moore; illustrated by Paul Doherty.– [Revised ed.]
p. cm.
Includes index.
Summary: Takes the reader on a tour of the solar system, describing the sun, planets,
comets, asteroids, and meteors.
ISBN 0-7613-0825-3
1. Solar system–Juvenile literature. 2. Astronomy–Juvenile literature.
[1. Solar system. 2. Astronomy.] I. Doherty, Paul. ill. II. Title.
QB501.3.M66 1999
523.2–dc21
99-40547   CIP

My grateful thanks are due to Paul Doherty for his splendid pictures,
and to Lynn Lockett for all her help and encouragement.   P.M.

Patrick Moore
The Starry Sky

Illustrated by Paul Doherty

COPPER BEECH BOOKS
BROOKFIELD, CONNECTICUT

Contents

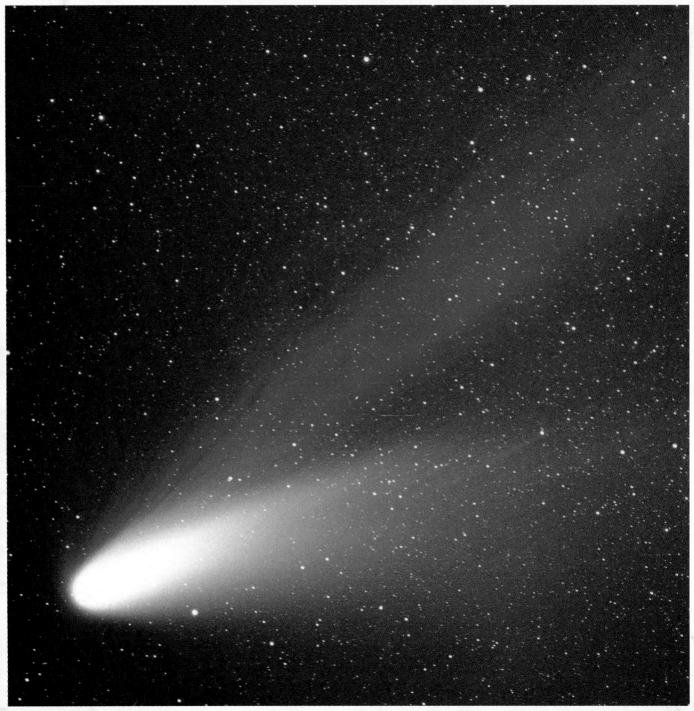

Foreword

Have you ever looked up into the sky and started to think about what you can see there? The sun, the moon, and the stars shine down, but not everyone takes the trouble to find out just what they are. I was six years old when I began to take an interest in them. In this book I have done my best to help you in making a start, and I hope that you will be interested enough to go on and make a real hobby out of astronomy. If you do I am sure that you will enjoy it, because there is so much to see, and there is always something new to find out. I wish you the best of luck!

Patrick Moore

The sun and the moon as seen from Earth.

The sun and its family

All our light comes from the sun. It is so bright that you must never look straight at it or you will hurt your eyes badly. The sun is much bigger than

the Earth, and it is a very long way away. The Earth moves around the sun, taking one year to make the full journey. There are eight other bodies of the same kind, which we call planets. Some of the planets have moons; we have one, our own moon, which shines because it is being lit up by the sun. As well as the planets and their moons, there are many bodies in the sun's family, and I will talk about all of these in this book.

Moon

Earth

gravity will not let it go. The air around us is made up of gas. If you swing your hand, you can feel the air being pushed out of the way. But the air does not spread upward forever. The higher you go, the less air there will be. On the tops of some mountains, the air is so thin that you could not breathe it. Out in space there is no air at all.

Mountaineers need to wear oxygen masks when they are very high up.

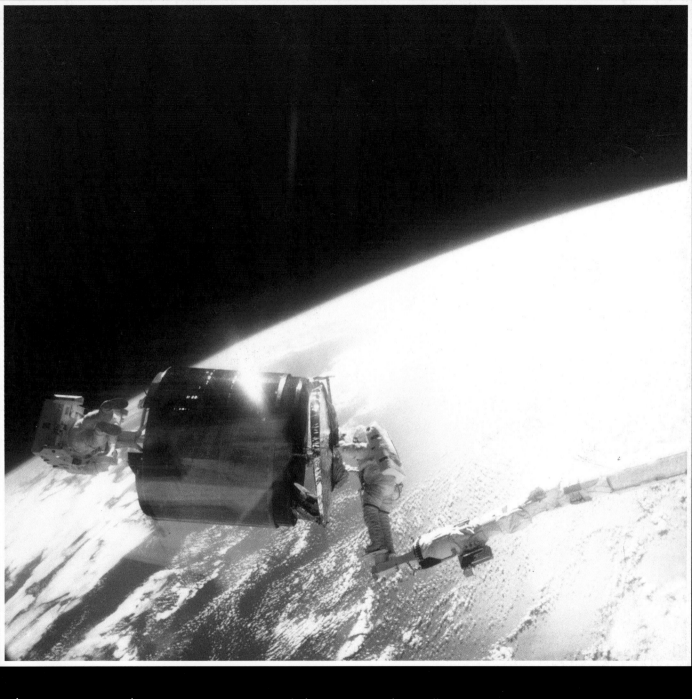

When you are traveling in space, you seem to have no weight at all.

Sometimes you can see the moon in the daytime sky.

The sun and moon in the sky

When it is daytime, and there are no clouds, you can see the sun. At night you can often see the moon. But do you know what the sun and the moon are really like? The sun is the larger of the two, but the moon is much closer to us. You already know that the Earth moves around the sun. The moon moves around the Earth, taking just over 27 days to do so.

The moon has no light of its own, and shines only because it is being lit up by the sun.

Looking at the sun and moon

The sun is very hot. If you hold out your hand to the sun, you will feel the heat. The sun is also very bright. You must never look straight at the sun. Astronomers use solar telescopes which reflect an image of the sun. The moon sends us almost no heat. You can look straight at the moon for as long as you like and you will not hurt your eyes.

Here an astronomer is measuring the sizes and positions of sunspots, using a very large telescope. Even then, the astronomer must wear dark glasses to make sure that he does not hurt his eyes.

Heat from the sun is so strong that it can quickly burn your skin.

How the sun moves

The Earth turns around once every 24 hours, so that to us it seems that the sky moves from east to west – taking the sun, the moon, and the stars with it. This is why the sun seems to rise in the east and set in the west every day.

Summer sun

The sun is higher in the sky in summer than in winter, which is why the days in summer are so warm. When the sun is low in the sky, its light comes to us through a thicker part of the Earth's air. This makes the sun look orange or red. Even then you must never look straight at it. Do not forget this; you must not hurt your eyes.

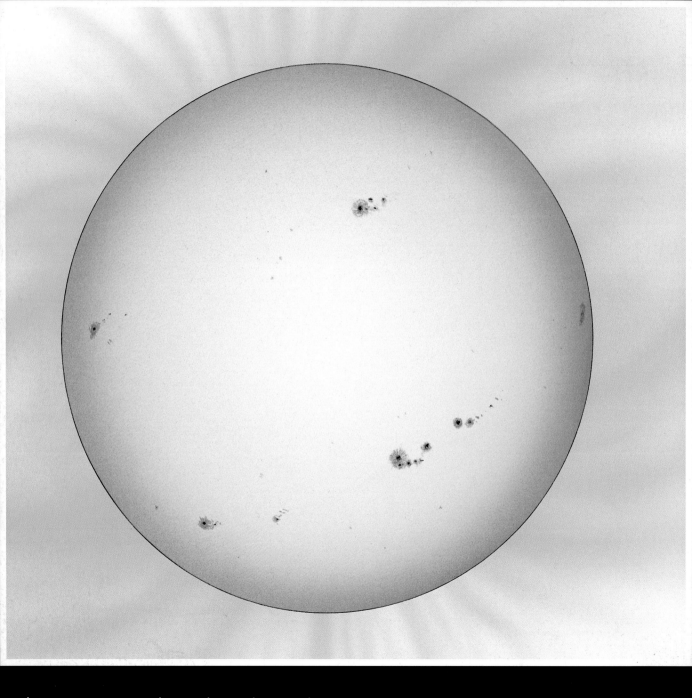

Dark "sunspots" are cooler patches in the sun's hot gas.

Spots on the sun

The sun is much, much bigger than the Earth. It is not solid, but is made up of gas, so you could not go there even if it were not so hot! Like the Earth, it is spinning around, but it takes nearly four weeks to make one full turn instead of only 24 hours. Sometimes there are dark patches on the sun. These patches are called sunspots. They look black because they are not as hot as the gas around them. They do not last for more than a few days or a few weeks, and at times there may be no sunspots at all.

How the sun shines

The sun is not burning in the same way as a fire. It is much hotter than any of the fires we have in our homes. Inside the sun, one kind of gas is changing into a different kind of gas, and this process is what makes the sun shine. The sun is very old – much older than the Earth – and it hardly changes at all. If it became even a little hotter or a little cooler, the Earth would become either too warm or too cold for us to live here.

The sun's heat is much weaker at the Earth's poles, so the climate there is cold.

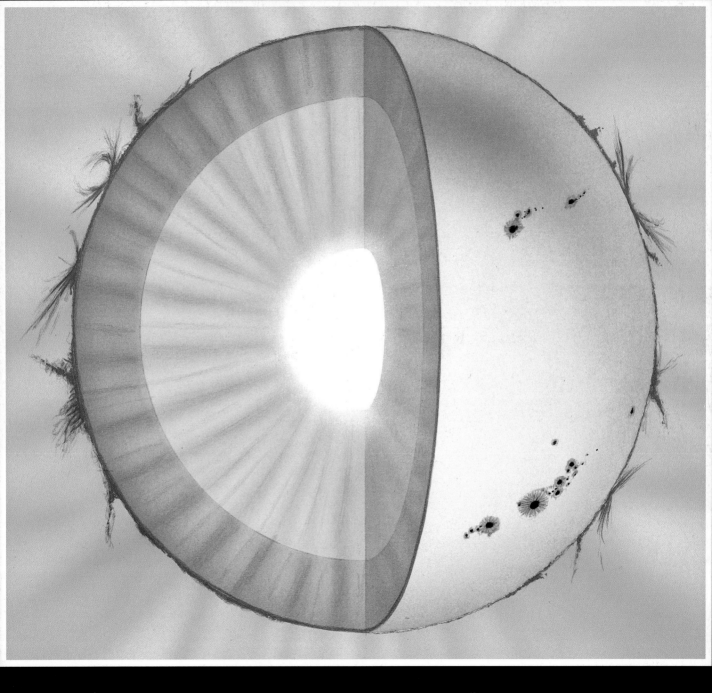

The sun is much hotter inside than it is at its surface.

Hide and seek

Sometimes the sun, the moon, and the Earth move into a straight line, with the

moon in the middle. When this happens, the moon hides the sun for a short time. That is what we call an eclipse.

When the moon is right in front of the sun, and hides the bright face, we can see the sun's outer gas, which spreads out across the sky. We cannot see the gas except at the time of an eclipse, because the sky is too bright.

Eclipses like this do not happen often. The next one can be seen from the United States on August 21, 2017. Perhaps you will be lucky enough to see it!

AUG
21
2017

How the moon moves

The sun can shine on only half of the moon at once, so that one half of the moon is bright and the other half is dark. This is why the moon seems to change shape. When the moon is almost between the Earth and the sun, its dark side is turned toward us, and we cannot see the moon at all; this is called new moon.

New moon

Quarter moon

As the moon moves in its path, we begin to see a little of the bright side; then we see half of the bright side, and at full moon the whole bright side faces us. Because the moon takes just over 27 days to go once around the Earth, we usually see one new moon and one full moon in every month.

Half moon

Full moon

The face of the moon

When you look at the moon, you can see bright and dark patches. The dark patches are called seas, but they are not real seas; there is no water in them – and in fact there is no water anywhere on the moon. There are high mountains, and there are many craters, which are really holes with walls around them.

The moon's rocky surface

Some people say that the dark patches look rather like a human face – you may have heard of the Man in the Moon. But there are no men on the moon, because there is no air, and without air no one can breathe.

28

The "seas" on the moon are low-lying plains.

29

A view of the Earth as it appears from the moon.

On the moon

If you could go to the moon, you would find that the sky is black even in the daytime. Because there is no air, there are no clouds and no wind; of course it never rains on the moon. The days are much longer than ours. From the moon you would be able to see the sun and the stars. You would also see the Earth, which would look much bigger and brighter than the moon does to us. Sometimes the Earth would be new, sometimes half and sometimes full, just as we see the moon.

Going to the moon

There is no air between the Earth and the moon, so that to go there it is necessary to use rockets, which can fly into empty space. Twelve men have been to the moon; the first man to land there was Neil Armstrong, in 1969. Since then rockets have been sent to the moon, but have carried no passengers. Plans are being made to set up a proper station there, and it is possible that you will be able to go to the moon one day, though when you are on the moon you will have to wear a spacesuit whenever you go outside the moon station.

There is no air on the moon so astronauts have to wear a special spacesuit.

The planets

The Earth's moon is not the only moon – just as the Earth is not the only planet. There are eight other planets, all moving around the sun. Some of these planets have moons of their own.

The closest planet to the sun is Mercury. Then comes Venus, our own Earth, and Mars, all of which are quite small. Further

Mercury

Venus

Earth

Mars

Asteroids

away than Mars there is a wide gap in which we find thousands of very small worlds which we call minor planets or asteroids.

Pluto

Neptune

Saturn

Jupiter

Uranus

Beyond those are four very big planets, Jupiter,

Saturn, Uranus, and Neptune, with one small planet,

Pluto. If you want to know the sizes of the planets, and

the times they take to go around the sun, look at pages

92-93 of this book.

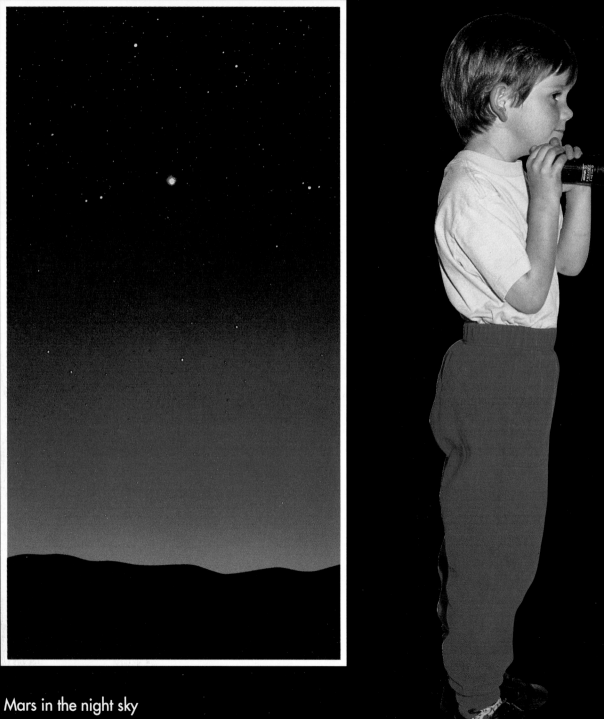

Mars in the night sky

Looking at the planets

Like the moon, the planets have no light of their own. We can see them because they are being lit up by the sun, just as you can light up a ball in a dark room by shining a lamp on it.

The stars are much like the sun, and are very hot, but they seem much less bright than the sun because they are further away. The planets look like stars, but they are really very different, and are much closer than any of the stars. They move slowly around in the sky, and this is how people first found out that they are not at all like the stars.

How the planets move

All the planets go around the sun; the closer ones move much more quickly than those which are further away. The Earth takes one year (365 days) to go once around the sun, but Mercury takes only 88 days, while Pluto takes 248 years. If you could live on Pluto, you would have to wait 248 years for your first birthday!

1 Mercury
2 Venus
3 Earth
4 Mars
5 Asteroids
6 Jupiter
7 Saturn
8 Uranus
9 Neptune
10 Pluto

Venus, Mars, Jupiter, and Saturn are so bright that you can find them easily. Mercury always stays close to the sun. You can barely see Uranus but the last two planets, Neptune and Pluto, are so faint that you cannot see them at all unless you use a telescope.

Going to the planets

Although twelve men so far have been to the moon, nobody has yet been to any of the planets. It would take a very long time to get there. But rockets have been sent past all the planets except Pluto, and have sent back pictures of them, so at least we know what they are like.

I am sure you have seen firework rockets. Rockets of this kind work in just the same way as the rockets which have been sent into space, but the spacerockets have very powerful rocket motors – otherwise they would not be able to go fast enough to escape from the Earth's gravity.

The Shuttle taking off in 1997

The hot planets

The first two planets, Mercury and Venus, are very hot. It is not easy to see Mercury, because it always stays so close to the sun. It is small, and has no air, so nobody could live there.

Mercury

The next planet, Venus, is nearly as big as the Earth. It can be very bright, and you can often see it in the west after sunset or in the east before the sun rises. It has very thick air, which we could not breathe, and it is so hot that any water there would boil away. It will be a long time before anyone can go to Venus for a visit.

Venus

43

44

<u>The red planet</u>

The first planet beyond the Earth is Mars. It is very red, and it is smaller than the Earth, though bigger than the moon. By using telescopes, which make faraway things seem closer, we can see that Mars has ice at its poles, just as the Earth has. There are no seas, and it is always very cold; the air

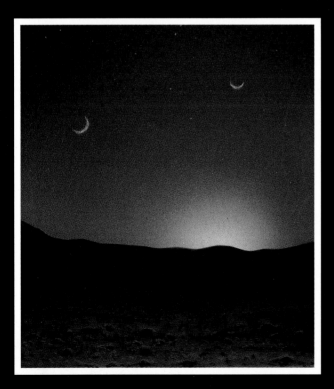

is so thin that we could not breathe it. Mars has two moons. Both are very small, and not at all like our moon. All the same it would be odd to see two moons in the sky, but neither would give off much light, and the nights on Mars will be much darker than ours.

View from the surface of Mars

Visiting Mars

No space travelers have yet been to Mars, but rockets have been sent there. In 1976 two rockets, called Vikings, landed in one of the red deserts and sent back pictures of the rocks and the sky, which is pink instead of blue. In 1997 another spacecraft, Pathfinder, landed on Mars; it was covered with an air bag, so that on landing it bounced! It carried a small vehicle, no bigger than a

Rockets were sent to take pictures of Mars.

television set, which moved around and proved that there had once

been water on Mars, though there are no seas there

now. Another spacecraft is still going around Mars

and sending back pictures. There are no people or

animals on Mars, but we are doing our best to find

out if there are any signs of life. Before long, we should be able to

set up a proper station there, inside which people can live and work.

The small vehicle called Sojourner could be commanded from Earth to move around and study the surface

The biggest planet Jupiter

Europa

is the biggest planet, and you can see it clearly for part of every year; it is much brighter than any of the stars. It takes nearly twelve years to go around the sun, but it has a very short day, less than ten hours long Ganymede

Jupiter is not like the Earth. Its surface is made up of gas, so we could never land a rocket there.

48

On Jupiter we can see lines, which we Io

call cloud belts. We can also see the

Great Red Spot, which is a huge storm in

Jupiter's gas.

Jupiter has 16 moons, and of these, four

are big. One of them,

called Ganymede, is

even bigger than

the planet

Mercury. You

can see these

four moons with

any telescope.

Callisto

Jupiter

The planet with the rings

The next planet is called Saturn. It is smaller than Jupiter, but much bigger than the Earth, and looks like a bright star in the sky.

Like Jupiter, Saturn has a surface made up of gas. It is very beautiful, because it has rings around it, though you cannot see them without a telescope. The rings are made up of little bits of ice moving around Saturn.

Saturn has 18 known moons, although astronomers suspect there may be more, at least three or perhaps even as many as seven. One of Saturn's moons, Titan, has thick air, though it is so cold that we could not live there.

Saturn's rings are made of pieces of ice.

51

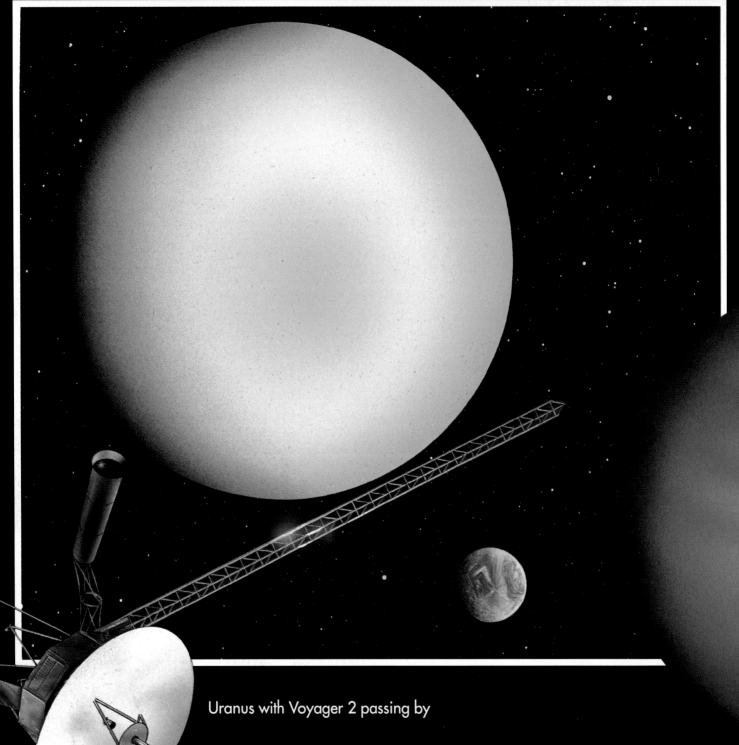

Uranus with Voyager 2 passing by

52

<u>Very cold planets</u> The last

three planets are so far away that they look

faint. Uranus and Neptune are about half as big

as Saturn, and both have moons. Uranus has 15 moons;

Pluto

Neptune, eight. Uranus is green; Neptune, blue. A spaceship

called Voyager 2 passed by them both, so we have

good pictures of them.

Pluto is smaller than our moon, and no

spaceship has yet reached it. It is so cold

that air of the kind we know would

freeze. If you could go to Pluto, the sun

would look only like a very bright star.

Now that you know what you are looking

for, go outdoors at night and find the closer

Neptune

planets for yourself!

53

Tail   Ice

Core

Comets

Comets move around the sun, but they are not like the Earth and the other planets. A comet is made up of a lump of ice, mixed with dust. As it moves through space, it leaves a trail of "dust" behind it, and it is these pieces of "dust" that we see as shooting stars, or meteors, as they fall into the Earth's air.

A comet is a long way away, so that it does not move quickly across the sky in the same way as a meteor. You have to watch a comet for many hours before you can see that it has moved at all.

Shooting stars are left behind by comets.

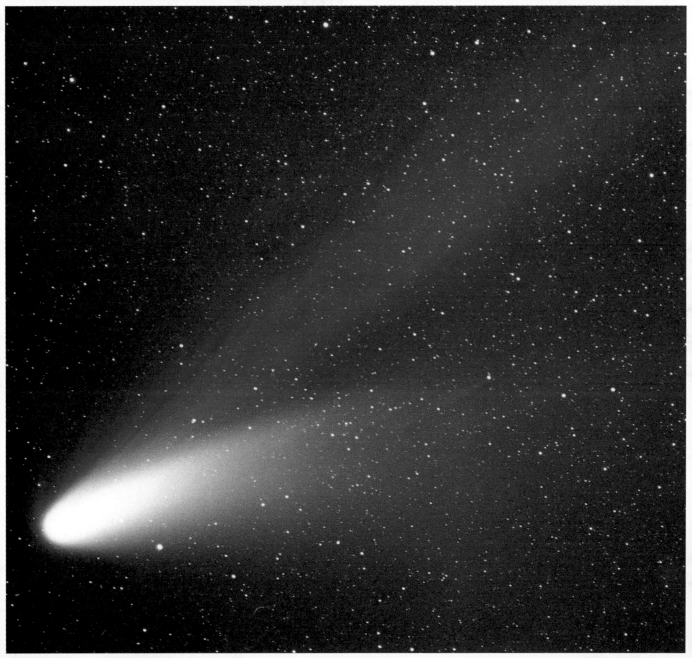

The comet's tail points
away from the sun.

ORBIT OF THE COMET

How comets move The Earth

Earth

goes around the sun in almost a circular path. A

comet has a different sort of path. As you can see from the picture,

a comet may sometimes be much closer to the sun than we are,

while at other times it will be much farther away. Some comets take

only a few years to go once around the sun, but others take a very long time indeed – many hundreds or even thousands of years.

A comet shines because it is being lit up by the sun, so it is bright only when it is close to us. When it is a long way away, it becomes so faint that we cannot see it at all.

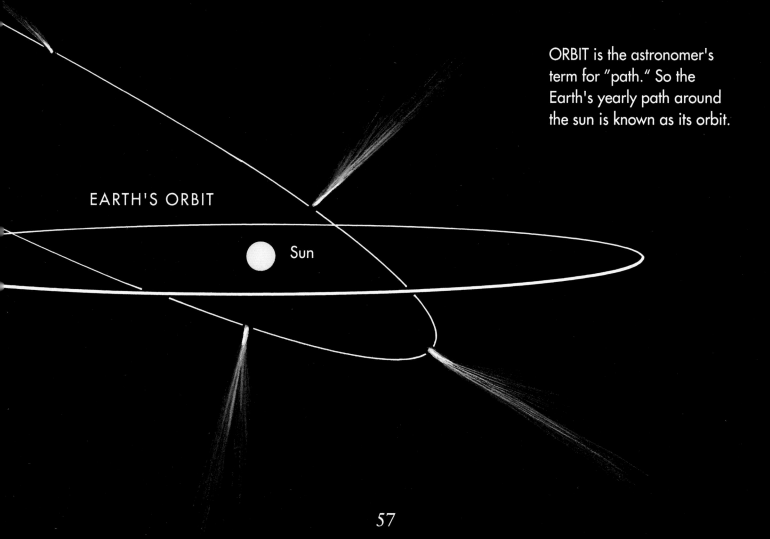

ORBIT is the astronomer's term for "path." So the Earth's yearly path around the sun is known as its orbit.

EARTH'S ORBIT

Sun

Halley's Comet The best-known

comet is called Halley's Comet, after an astronomer named

Edmond Halley who first found out that it moves around the sun. It

appears on the average every 75 years, and has been seen very

often; it was in the sky just before the Battle of Hastings, in 1066,

when William the Conqueror landed in England!

The Bayeux Tapestry, showing Halley's Comet, is 900 years old.

When it last came back, in 1986, five spaceships

were sent to it, and one of them went right through the comet's

head, sending back pictures of the icy lump in the middle.

Halley's Comet has now moved away from the sun, and is too

faint to be seen, but we know where it is. When it comes back, in the

year 2061, you may be lucky enough to see it for yourself.

Halley's Comet passing the space probe Giotto

Shooting stars

Meteors come from comets. If you are looking into the sky on a dark night, when there are no clouds, you may sometimes see a streak of light which moves quickly across the night sky. This is what we call a meteor, or shooting star. It is not at all like a real star; it is only a tiny piece of "dust" burning away in the Earth's upper air. Some meteors may become very bright, but they do not last for more than a few seconds before they disappear. They burn away long before they can fall to the ground.

What makes a shooting star?

A meteor moves around the sun in the same way as the Earth does. When it is in space, we cannot see it, because it is much too small. We see it only when it moves into the top of the Earth's air, and becomes hot because of what we call friction.

If you pump up a bicycle tire, you will find that the pump gets hot, because the air inside it is being squashed; this causes friction, which causes heat. A meteor moving into the upper air creates so much heat by friction against the air that it catches fire, and burns away.

Showers of shooting stars

Meteors usually move around the sun in bunches. When the Earth moves through one of these bunches, it collects many pieces of "dust," and the result is a shower of shooting stars.

This happens several times in every year, but the best time to see meteors is in the first part of August, when the Earth passes through a dense bunch. If you look up into a dark, clear sky for a few minutes at any time between the end of July and about August 17, you will probably be lucky enough to see several shooting stars. Of course, you can see them at other times; meteors may appear at any moment.

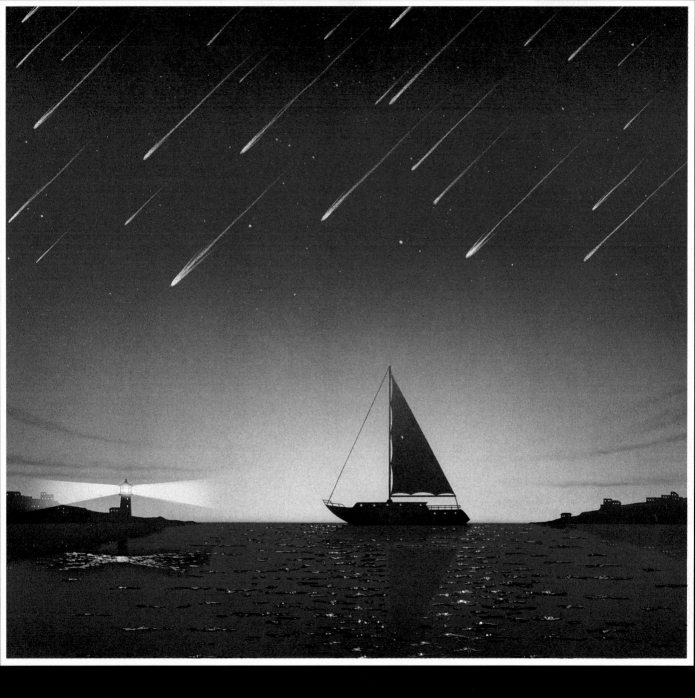

A shower of shooting stars

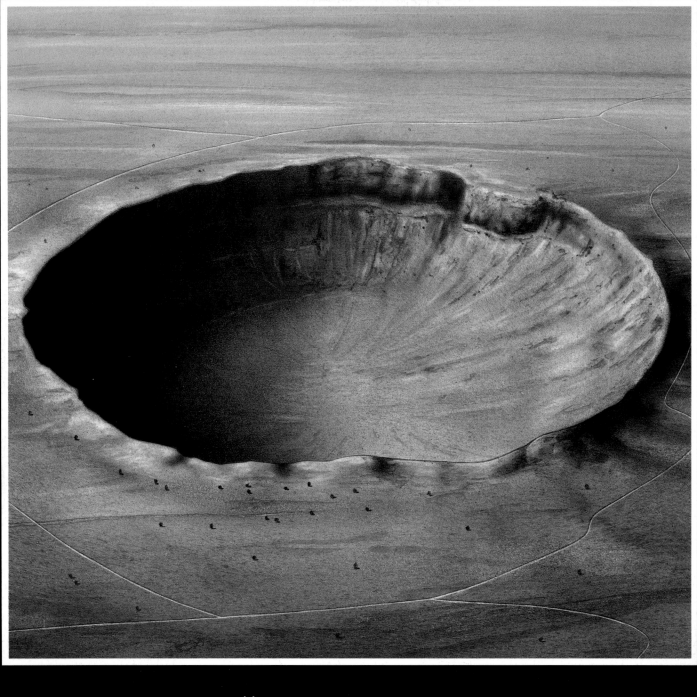

Large meteorite crater in Canyon Diablo, Arizona

Stones from space

Sometimes the Earth meets a body which is big

enough to drop right through the air without being burned away. It

then lands on the Earth, and is called a meteorite.

Museums keep collections of meteorites; you can see them there.

Most are made up of stone and iron. They do not come from

comets, and are quite different from shooting star meteors.

A large meteorite may make a large hole or

crater; one of these craters, in Arizona, is

nearly a mile wide. If a populated area of the

Earth were hit by a body of this kind there

would be a great deal of damage, but luckily

it is not likely to happen. Nobody has ever been killed by a stone

falling from space, so you can feel quite safe when you go outdoors

Looking at the stars

When you look up into the sky at nighttime, you will also see the stars. There are so many stars that you would find it impossible to count them all. Some are very bright; others are dim.

You cannot see the stars in the daytime, because the sky is too bright, but they are always there. As soon as the sun has set and the sky has become dark, the stars begin to show. They seem to twinkle, but this is only because the light from them has to come through the air above us. If the Earth had no air, the stars would not twinkle at all.

The sky looks very different at nighttime.

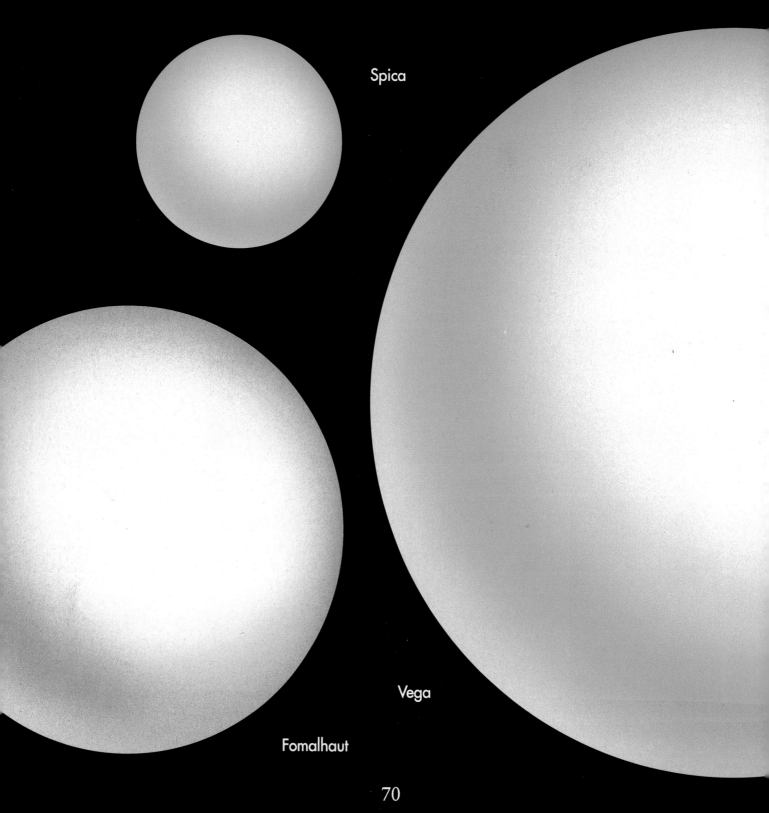

Spica

Fomalhaut

Vega

What the stars are like

The stars look like tiny lamps in the sky, but they are really very big and hot. The sun, which sends us all our light and heat, is only a star.

The Earth moves around the sun, which looks much brighter than any of the other stars because it is much closer to us. The sun is much bigger than the Earth, but we know that some of the stars are much bigger and hotter than the sun. The stars look so small and faint because they are such a long way away from us.

Our sun

How the stars seem to move

If you watch the night sky, you will see all the stars moving very slowly across the sky from east to west. But they are not really moving like this. They seem to do so because the Earth is turning around; this makes the sky seem to move, carrying all the stars with it.

The stars are not fixed in the sky. All of them are moving around, but they are so far away from us that they always appear to be in the same groups.

The stars we see now look just the same as they did 2,000 years ago. Even their light takes many years to reach us, so that we do not see them as they are "now;" we see them as they used to be years ago!

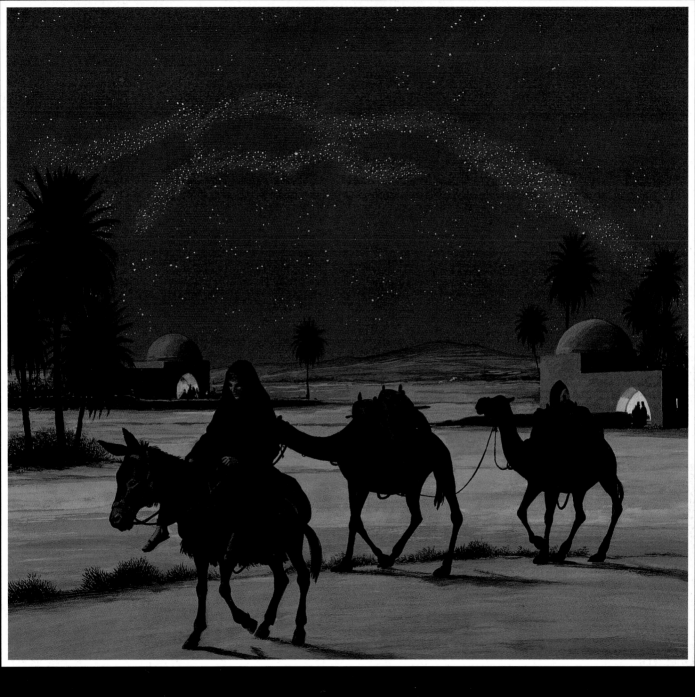

The night sky in this scene of long ago would look no different today.

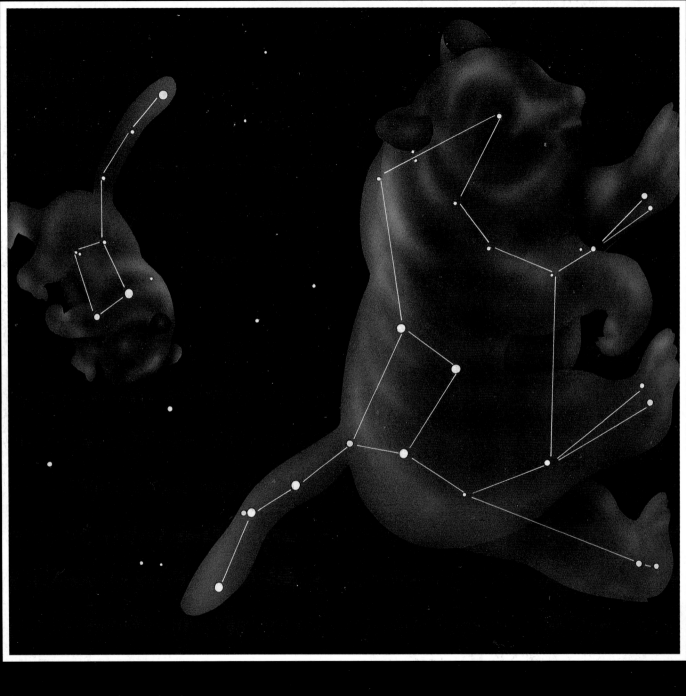

The two Bears in the night sky

The two bears in the sky

People who lived long ago gave names to the groups of stars, and made up stories about them. One of these stories was about two bears, who were pulled up by their tails and put into the sky. The Great Bear, sometimes called the Big Dipper, is shown by seven stars which make a shape which is very easy to find. The Little Bear is not so bright, but in it we find the North Pole of the sky, close to the North Star. Once you have found the North Star you will always be able to find it again, because it does not seem to move at all.

In Australia or New Zealand, the Great Bear is very low in the sky, and you cannot see the Little Bear at all. You can see new groups, such as the Southern Cross, which are only visible in a few places in the United States.

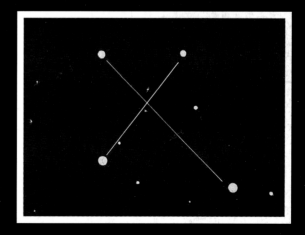

The Southern Cross

The hunter and his dog

Another story is about a hunter who said that he could kill any animal he met. His name was Orion, and his stars are much brighter than those of the two Bears. You cannot always see Orion, because he is in the night sky for only part of the year. Orion is high up when it is winter in the United States, and summer in Australia. In Orion there are two very bright stars called Betelgeux and Rigel, and three stars in a line which make up the Hunter's Belt.

The Great Dog

Not far from Orion is the Great Dog, in which we find the brightest of all the nighttime stars. Its name is Sirius, but most people just call it the Dog Star. Further south is another very bright star, Canopus, which can never be seen from the United States. In Australia you can see Canopus in the night sky for most of the year.

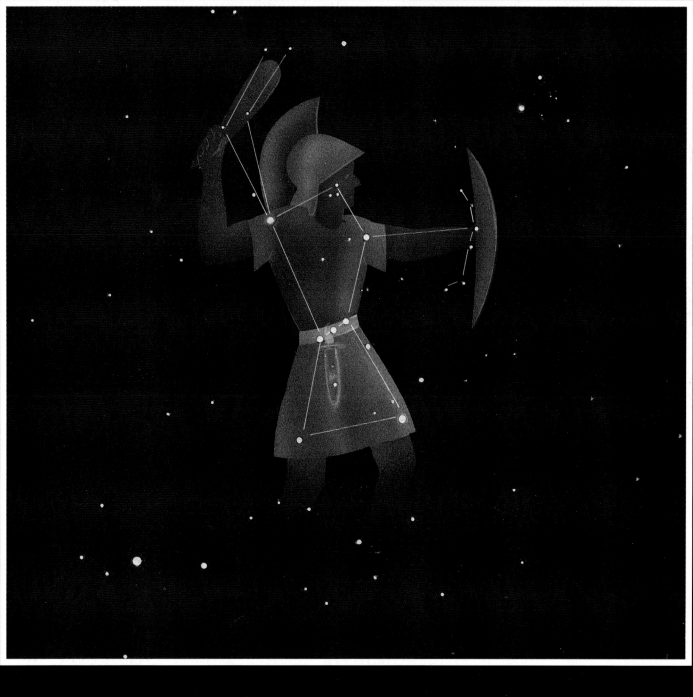

Orion with the two stars Betelgeux and Rigel

The colors of the stars

White star (Sirius)

If you look at the stars, you will see that they are not all the same color. Our sun is yellow; most of the nighttime stars look white, but there are a few which are orange or red. This is because some of the stars are hotter than others.

White stars are hotter than yellow stars, while yellow stars are hotter than those which are orange or red. Most of the stars in Orion are white, but there is one which is red; this is the one named Betelgeux, but it is often called "Beetle-juice!"

78

Yellow star
(Our sun)

Red star
(Betelgeux)

Orange star
(Aldebaran)

79

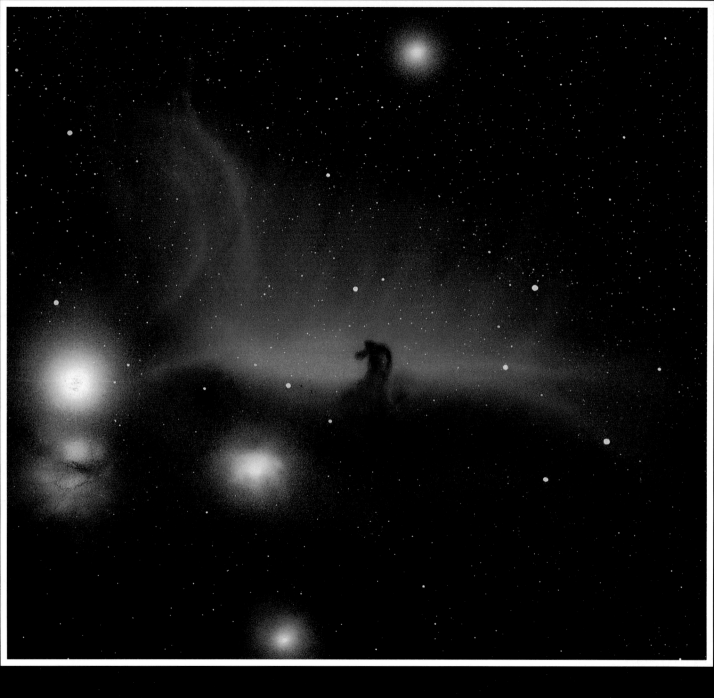

The Horsehead Nebula

How stars are born Here

and there in the night sky we can see patches of

dust and gas. There is a special name for them; they

are called "nebulae" (pronounced neb-you-lee), from an old word

which means "clouds." Inside these clouds, new stars are being born.

Long ago, our sun was born in just the same way.

Some of the nebulae

are easy to find.

There is one in the

star group of Orion

the Hunter; you can

see it near the three

bright stars which

make up the

Hunter's Belt.

The Great Nebula in Orion, M42

How stars die

The sun, like all the other stars, cannot live forever. When it can no longer shine, it will become very dark and heavy, and then it will become cold and dark. Luckily this will not happen for a very long time, so there is no need to worry about the sun going out. For many millions of years the sun will look just the same as it does now.

Some very big stars do not live for so long, and when they can no longer shine they blow up! Sometimes we can see a star doing this. For a few days or weeks it may be very bright, but before long it fades away.

But remember that the light from the stars takes years to reach us, so that when we watch a star blowing up we are seeing something which really happened a long time ago.

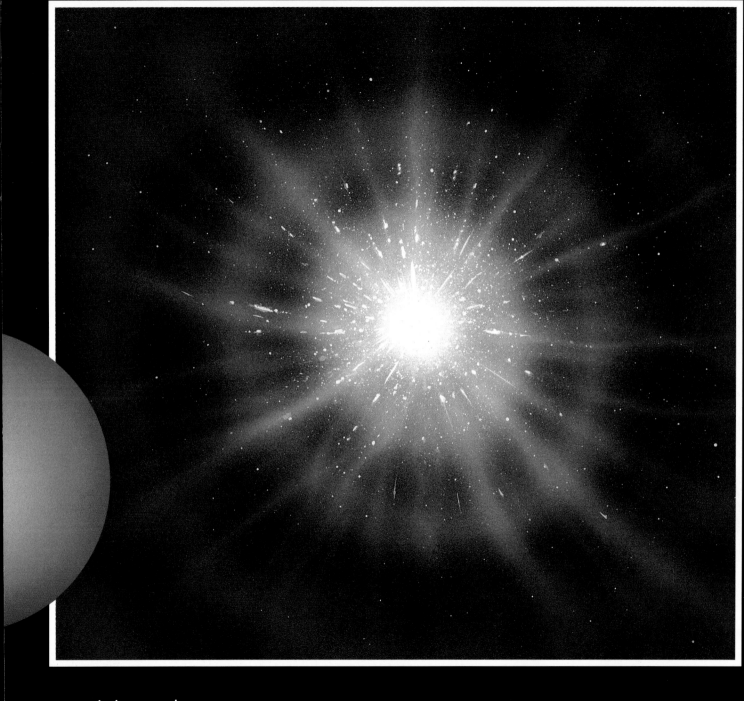

An exploding star, known as a supernova

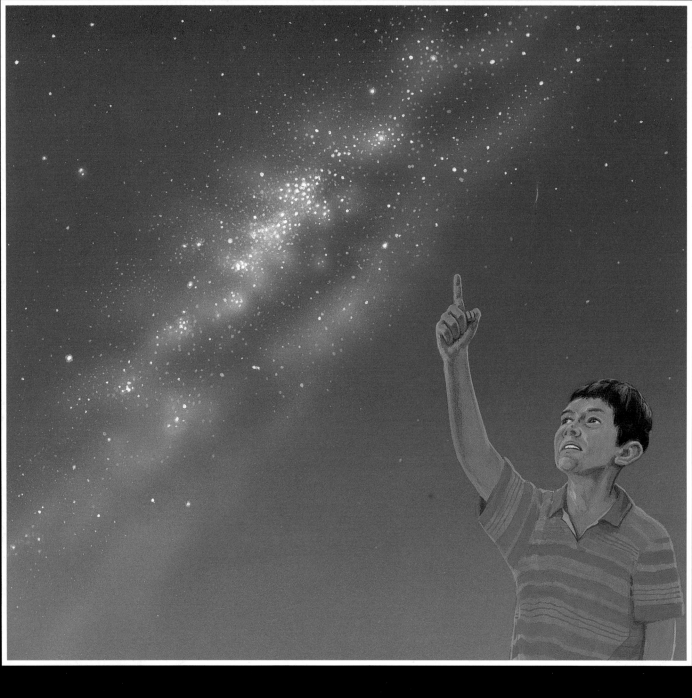

The Milky Way in the night sky

The Milky Way

If you live away from a town, and there are no lights near you, you will be able to see the Milky Way. This looks like a band of light crossing the night sky. It is made up of stars which look as if they are very close together.

This is not really true. The system of stars in which we live is shaped just like two fried eggs put together back-to-back. When we look along the thick part of the system, we can see many stars, almost one behind the other, and it is this which makes up the Milky Way.

Side view
of our galaxy

We have a special name for the system of stars in which we live; we call it the galaxy. In it there are at least a hundred billion stars.

Other galaxies The

S-shaped galaxy

Milky Way galaxy is not the only

one. There are many others.

Most of them are so far

away that their light

takes millions of years to reach us. We

also know that except for a few of the

closer galaxies, all of them are moving

away from us, so that the whole universe

is spreading out. Many of the galaxies

Elliptical galaxy

are what we call "spirals,"

as shown in the picture; in

fact our own galaxy is a spiral,

and the sun, together with the Earth,

lies near the edge of one of the spiral arms.

Top view of our galaxy as it would be seen from a spacecraft a million light years away. The arrow points to our Earth.

Getting to know the stars

When you first look up into a sky which seems to be full of stars, you may think that you will never be able to tell one from another. But because the stars are so far away, the groups do not change, and this makes it easy to learn your way around.

A group of stars is called a "constellation," but the stars in any constellation are not really close to each other; they are at very different distances from us, so that one star in a constellation may be a long way "behind" another.

Soon you will recognize different constellations. You will be able to find the Bears, Orion the Hunter, and all the others visible from your part of the Earth. You will be able to see the red and orange stars, the gas clouds and much more. If you take a star map and go out at night, you will quickly find that you are making friends with all the stars.

The Hubble Space Telescope can see a very long way into space.

Other Earths?

Although our star, the sun, has eight other planets besides the Earth moving around it, we could not live on any of them. Some are too hot; others are too cold, and they do not have the right sort of air for us to breathe. But it may well be that other stars have planets of their own, with life on them.

If this is true – and we cannot be sure! – then there may be people like ourselves. We cannot send spaceships to planets of other stars, because they are too far away,

but one day we may be able to find out that we are not alone in space. Whether this happens or not, we may be sure that in the next few years we are going to discover many new and exciting facts about space and our universe.

Here are some facts about the planets

which you may like to know.

MERCURY
36
88 days
58 days
3,030
0

VENUS
67
225 days
243 days
7,520
0

EARTH
93
365¼ days
24 hours
7,925
1

MARS
142
687 days
24½ hours
4,220
2

JUPITER
483
11¾ years
9¾ hours
88,740
16

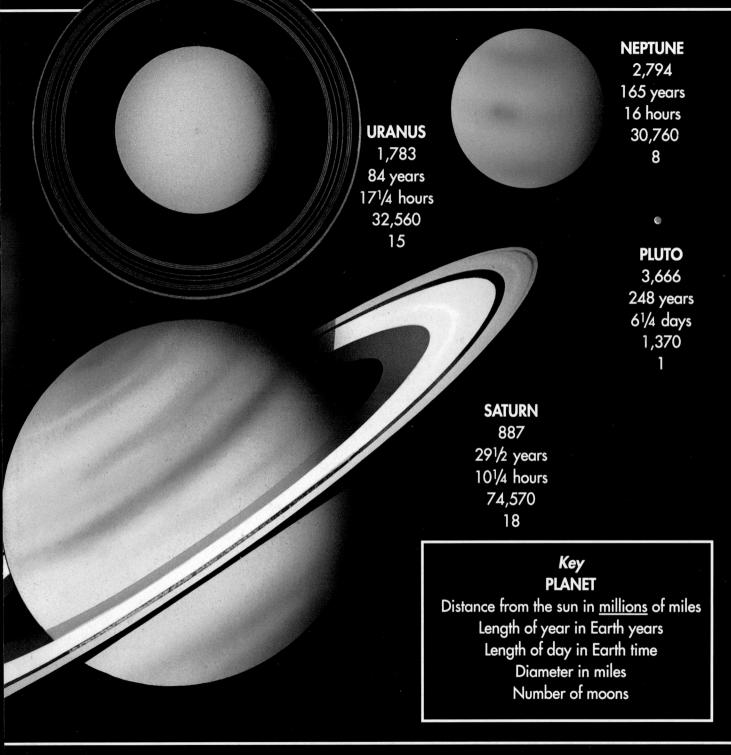

NEPTUNE
2,794
165 years
16 hours
30,760
8

URANUS
1,783
84 years
17¼ hours
32,560
15

PLUTO
3,666
248 years
6¼ days
1,370
1

SATURN
887
29½ years
10¼ hours
74,570
18

Key
PLANET
Distance from the sun in <u>millions</u> of miles
Length of year in Earth years
Length of day in Earth time
Diameter in miles
Number of moons

Index